鶴

THE CRANE

First published in 2022 by
The Dedalus Press
13 Moyclare Road
Baldoyle
Dublin D13 K1C2
Ireland

www.dedaluspress.com

ISBN 978-1-910251-94-2 (paperback)
ISBN 978-1-910251-95-9 (hardback)

Dedalus Press titles are available in Ireland
from Argosy Books (www.argosybooks.ie) and in the UK
from Inpress Books (www.inpressbooks.co.uk)

Cover image: iStockPhoto.com

The Dedalus Press receives financial assistance from
The Arts Council / An Chomhairle Ealaíon.

the arts council
chomhairle
ealaíon
funding
literature
artscouncil.ie

LITERATURE
IRELAND
Promoting and Translating Irish Writing

鶴

THE CRANE

Selected Poems of Yau Noi

TRANSLATED BY

Liu Xun and Harry Clifton

DEDALUS PRESS

Contents

FOREWORD

Chinese literature has always been almost too immense to talk about, for myself or for many lecturers working in institutions outside of China. It's a literature that has witnessed more than five thousand years of social, political, as well as historical change. If a lecturer chooses to lecture on the subject, what must be included on the syllabus? Mythology, classical poetry from ancient times to the 1900s, essays by literates of all dynasties, vernacular novels, modern poetry, contemporary novels? Fortunately, the present project offered a clearer path, as there is no need to scope out such immensity but only to focus on four decades of time.

That said, to offer some context on modern Chinese poetry, I would like to elaborate on its historical evolution and how it relates to classical Chinese poetry, that is poetry written in Classical Chinese and typified by certain traditional forms and genres. As modern Chinese poetry was part of the language evolution, I will begin with a brief introduction to classical Chinese poetry. Classical Chinese poetry is traditional Chinese poetry written in Classical Chinese and typified by certain traditional forms and genres. The existence of classical Chinese poetry can be traced back to 1100 BC, which can be documented by the publication of *Shi Jing (Classic of Poetry)*. Over the ages, various forms and genres have been adopted. Today, the most well-known forms are Han Fu, Tang Shi, and Song Ci (folk ballads, romantic poetry, and poems intended for singing, respectively). Modern Chinese poetry, including new poetry (新诗) or modern vernacular poetry (白话诗), mostly refers to post Qing Dynasty poetry. Modern Chinese poetry became increasingly popular with the New Culture (文化运动) and 4th May (五四运动) movements. As an alternative to the traditional poetry written in classical Chinese, experimental poetic styles and 'free verse' were adopted by many poets.

On one hand, four decades of time counts as nothing in the grand history of Chinese literature. On the other, four decades can be incredibly important to the story of modern Chinese literature. During these four decades, not only was a country's destiny reshaped but also millions of destinies were totally redirected. Our poet Yau Noi was one of those millions.

Yau Noi, also known as Wa Lan (a former pseudonym) comes from a small village in Jiangsu Province, Southern China. He was born in 1965; his birthplace, a farm in Linhai, was several hours' bike ride from the nearest bus station. During his years in junior high school, he fell in love with poetry and excelled in Chinese; the school principal encouraged him to represent his county by participating in the national writing contest. However, this did not change his fate. After graduating from high school, Yau Noi, like all his classmates, was not admitted to a university. Instead, he returned to Linhai and began to help his father to support the family by working on the family farm. He contracted 13 acres of rice fields and raised 8 black pigs. He picked two large buckets of pig food and walked a mile and a half to feed the pigs every day. Despite the exhausting and repetitive labour, he did not give up his dream of becoming a poet and read eagerly anything that could be accessed from an isolated farm. Under heavy manual labour, he was not giving up his dream to become a poet. He was eager to read anything that could be accessed from an isolated farm.

In 1984, Yau Noi finally had the opportunity to escape from farm life to work in a county town. In 1985, he read 'the Misty poets'[1] for the first time. Drawn by the fascinating world of poetry, he decided to quit his job to write. Later that year, Yau Noi went to Beijing. In Beijing, he joined the circle of poets and met Xuedi, Xing Tian, and Wei Mang, the main members

---

1 The Misty Poets (Chinese: 朦胧诗人; pinyin: Ménglóng Shīrén) are a group of 20th-century Chinese poets who reacted against the restrictions on art in the 1970s. They are so named as their works were officially denounced as "obscure", "misty", or "hazy".

of the 'Yuanmingyuan Poetry Society'.[2] His encounters with the Beijing poets during this period had a profound impact on him.

In terms of poetic content and aesthetic tendency, Yau Noi's poetry preserves the temperament of 'Misty Poetry', as well as the seeking of an ideal world. He also claims that he has been deeply influenced by Paul Celan. It was Celan who encouraged him to draw strength and poetic inspiration from suffering. This influence can be seen when we read his poetry recalling his childhood memories, especially from the lines talking about freezing winters and deformed body parts. Besides, from Celan's introduction, Yau Noi became interested in 'Russian poetry from the Silver Age'.[3] He once revealed his love for Osip Mandelstam. After leaving Beijing, Yau Noi met Cheng Shang in Nanjing. Under the influence of Cheng Shang, his poetry gradually developed a surrealist style, as we read nowadays.

For myself, I did not directly witness those great changes. When taking on this poetry translation, I felt I had to travel back with our poet to the winters of rural China, then to the exciting years in Beijing of the '80s and after, following a solo cosmopolitan wanderer to explore his world.

I often worked late into the night. Yau Noi is a poet of the emotions, but always grounded or earthed in his work. We have divided the poems of *The Crane* into three sections which, loosely, follow the three main 'movements' of the poet's writing life, 'Before', 'During' and 'After', the 'During' section inspired by and describing the profound changes that took place in China during the poet's early years. For me, the intensity of the emotions evoked was almost beyond my experience, especially in the poems from his early period. The three periods together describe a journey from 'the unbearable heaviness of being' to

----

2 Yuanmingyuan Poetry Society, a modern poetry society founded in 1984, Beijing.

3 The Silver Age of Russian poetry is an artistic period, it dates from late 19th century to the 1920s. It implies a wide range of poets, genres, and literary styles. It was an exceptionally creative period in the history of Russian poetry.

'the unbearable lightness of being.' From the perspective of Yau Noi, life can be as suffocating as the dense wintery fogs or as light as the cooking fumes above a heated pan.

In this sense, for me Yau Noi's *The Crane* is a history book. I was not so much a translator of words as a storyteller charged with retelling history for a new generation. I am obliged to my co-translator Harry Clifton for his help in ensuring that these stories are well retold.

— Liu Xun

鹤

梦的峭壁甜蜜环绕
风吹散黄昏与马匹
群山在我身后漫游

鹤示爱弯腰俯首

The Crane

Among dream-cliffs,
Storm-scatterings, horses of apocalypse,
Mountain ranges, times out of mind,

The crane bows down. The artist has signed.

Before

冬天

北方的冬天干燥枯寂，神秘的
乌鸦盘旋在山林
燕子沉默地飞出倒塌的墙角

田野很远，马车的铃铛在月色中摇响
你能想象车夫戴着厚重的皮帽
马蹄踏碎星辰

野兽躲在山后，受伤后一直流血
大地颤抖起来，小咏，你在哪？
孤独的旅行者，正漫步在你寂静的故乡

Winter

Winter in northern China, fogbound,
Swallowed in obscurantism.
Crows like overseers in the listening woods,
Sparrows without shelter, making themselves scarce.

And in the distance, the fields
In the moonlight, jingles of harness –
Can you hear it still?
The driver, with his great fur hat
Against the starry sky,

And the beasts, bleeding under the lash,
And the vast earth quaking.
Yong, where are you? In this
Your silent hometown, I who arrive
Am lonely for you.

我的童年

我的童年，经常被神灵救起
村里的大人骂我，老师用鞭子打我

人们讨厌我变蓝的脸

我走遍黑夜，坐在空地或河岸
幼兽在竹林翻刨新芽

林子里晨曦的空气清爽
愿望与髋骨生长。衰退腐烂……

神说：你们的信心在哪里呢
人性有多黑暗呢

Childhood

Blessed by divinity, spat on by villagers,
I was once a child.

Whipped by teachers, face turning blue,
I was once a child.

A child with an ugly mug, trespassing
On bare ground, river bank.

Young beasts were gouging out roots
In the bamboo forest smelling of freshness.

Morning grew in me, hard as desire,
As suddenly waned, decayed.

Where is my faith? How dark my majority?
I, once a child, afraid.

神迹

深夜举行的葬礼，是银河撒下的种子
黎明的蛋尚未破壳，在悬崖
没有桥通往死亡的深邃处

被遮掩的脊椎有一排笛孔，风吹散了年轮
溃散的黄昏落下无数纽扣
没有目的，没有去处

他是大地上的阴影，并不是神迹
早晨有时是一个瞬间，凋谢的花朵像肉体
它变得清晰时，又失去方向

Heavenly Sign

Funerals deep in the night
Are stars gone astray from their galaxy.

Dawn has yet to burst from its eggshell.
Nothing bridges the chasm of death.

Vertebrae, flute stops, burial mounds –
Trees disappearing in cosmic wind,

Dissolving dust, a darkness of clouds
Going nowhere, unreadable.

And He, a darkness shadowing earth
And never a sign from heaven.

借

借天。借居的大地倒塌又卷起
死亡前的死亡。是借来生活

光明坐在黑暗的怀里
她出现在你面前

春天。幽灵在月圆时分起舞
借来的书放在幽暗处
你问起春天时我想起出生的奥秘

On Lease

The sky has already been taken.
Life, like earth, is still on lease,
A crumbling of deaths into death.

Light surrounded by darkness –
Her shadow emerges, before our very eyes –
Primavera, spectral, turning under the full moon.

Primavera – when you name it
I see again the power of existence,
The borrowed book you now no longer need.

珏1985

在灰色的年代
鸟怀着海洋的孩子

农夫扛着稻谷
阳光在他笑脸上

生活，高贵腐烂的生活
你像一对冰凉的玉，
坠在我裤带上

Jade, 1985

That year, seabirds on grey,
Black and white morals blown away.

Peasants shouldering harvested grain,
Poster-smiles and hidden pain.

Hard truth, later to be felt
Like the piece of jade in my belt.

呼吸

春天来了。漫游者从南方来
她拜访过宫殿。
森林往南挪了挪

童年的呼吸像火苗。燕子像火苗
漂亮的小妹窥探陌生的禽兽
燕子总是忙个不停
小妹闪烁着。
星星凑近了餐桌和她的额头

Breaths

Wanderer of the south,
Coming from where Spring rests,
She pays us a visit in our palace
In the legendary forest.

Youngest of sisters, I am too old –
You alone can speak of her
And yourself, the life outside death,
The stars on the table, and maidenhead
In the same breath.

此刻，谁在海边哭泣

我从梦中惊醒，童年的村庄卷起
月亮领着它朝南飞。孤单的
丢失的玩具与搬走的邻居

秋天病了，战争将在冬天结束
鸟掌龙飞越大西洋，仅仅为最后一次繁殖
我哑了。
在岸边聆听风声回旋。

By the Sea

I was jolted from a dream
In which the village of my childhood
Appeared again to me.

Lost toys, the old neighbourhood
In decay, and the moon
In solitude, gone its own way.

Nature at war with itself
In a sick autumn, void of feeling –
Even the bird Ornithoceirus

Flown beyond Atlantics, on a last migration,
And myself, on the windswept shoreline,
Dumbstruck, listening.

四月莲花

我的爱人是纯净悠闲的莲花，
她坐在山坡上发呆时，
眼里有春天的景象。

她发芽如蔷薇，秃鹫在她头顶盘旋。
我嗅出神的气息，
从地下突然上升到这个世界。

Waterlily in April

My love
Is lying on a hillside, in a trance
As open-eyed as a waterlily
Taking in
The fullness of Spring

Exfoliating
Like a rambler rose
Over which
Birds of prey are circling

I smell the scent of immortal being
The beginning of death

三只鹅

三只鹅疲倦地坐在春天
生活被刮得不留一丁点肉，只剩下道德和骨头
诗人被排挤在生活之外

鲸鱼误入内地的浅滩
现在你可以呕吐，吐尽你所有憎恨
我刚刚来到这里，遇到了三只鹅

Three Geese

Three geese resting, on the groundlessness
Of Spring or Poetry
Call it what you will.

Life stripped to the bone,
Morality, like a stranded whale
Drowning in thin air,
Life without meaning, words gone stale,
Life with nothing to spare

But three geese resting, on the groundlessness
Of Spring or Poetry
And I approach them still.

太阳

动物在太阳下死去，女孩在太阳下练琴

太阳照常升起，树叶照常飘逝
上帝坐在何处？
天使飞到人间，它有温暖的翅膀
山的阴影里，受伤的动物一直流血

黄昏骑在马背上
只有你无需太阳，在一盏最小的灯下就能睡眠

Without Sun

Animals, nature, sun,
And a young girl playing a piano.

The sun rises, as it normally does.
The leaves fall, as they normally do.
The animals weaken and die
On the shadow side of the mountain.

And where, in all this,
Is the divinity? An angel,
A dusk arriving on horseback
Sweeping it all away.

All but the girl, who plays without light
Her piano, through the night.

列车经过黑夜的平原

山川草木飞进你身后的黑暗
世界在午夜旋转
远处幽暗的光，勾起碍难的童年

留在记忆的羊群
围攻过村庄？疯狂的是幽灵？
闪电在平原腹部留下深不可测的伤口

The Night Express

Mountains, grass and forest
Swallowed up in darkness, left behind.
My present elsewhere, past gone round the bend –
The dim lights in the distance, quivering,
The troubled childhood …

Flocks of goats, and the memory
Already vague, of villages under siege
And minds gone astray,
As lightning, in a snapshot of plain
Illuminates heartlands of pain.

During

最后一夜 1989

树叶卷起风，童话没了
只留下灰尘在尘世
坏人死在仇人的脑子里

而我们，自由的骑士与鼓手
往何处去？
越过人类未预感的道路

战马失明，天使用嘶哑的喉咙
喊我们掉头
扔掉盾牌，我们越过了黑暗的河流

The Last Night, 1989

We were blown leaves on the winds of time,
Dreamers, leaving a world behind
As different dreamers closed in for the kill.

What were our own dreams taking us to?
Liberal dreamers, marching to a different beat –
We called it victory, others defeat.

Mechanical warhorses, and the terrified screams
Of our own marshals, warning us back
As we walked on water, between two dreams.

字

造纸术让字繁衍。课本
被多次篡改。记忆伐光黑森林

他脸上有光
鸟往返于千年前树枝

字和字串通，捏造一个罪名
他被钉在集中营

Words

Words excused by the manufacture of paper
Textbooks censored a thousand times.

Memory, a blazing vision of someone's face,
Razed to the ground like charred forest.

Birds flitting between branches, ageless informers,
A bush telegraph of language, fabricating charges.

Words in collusion with words
Sending a man to prison, for rewards.

雪迪

我在夜里突然想起雪迪，诗人雪迪
写饥饿的雪迪，写颤栗的雪迪，
写骰子滚动的雪迪

他从冰上漂移到亮处
我们曾在云上行走，找最干净的词
生活在空虚中

他坐在悬崖上注视远方的峡谷
瀑布在他身后，原始的草地，北美的风

我的深夜正似他的黎明
走出树林的迷雾，倾听大海弯曲的秘密
在孤独的悬崖上，他寻找词语的桂冠

To Xue Di *

Xue Di, you come to mind
Suddenly, deep in the night,
You who write about hunger,
Fear, and the roll of the dice,

You melt, now, like light in ice,
Who strolled beside me once, on clouds,
Seeking the clearest of words
In the firmament, still alive,
Defying gravity ....

You look at the distanced valley,
Waterfalls left behind,
The grasslands of North America,
Your tanned face in the wind,

My midnight your sunrise
Now, in the misty wood,
On the heights grown sheer
With revelation, master of words,
And the oceans coming clear.

* *Xue Di is a Chinese poet (1957–)*

异乡人，请不要悲伤

大地倒下。踏上未知之路
人间让你有点不适
早起的智者惊醒鸟群

理想化为灰烬。
星空的马厩闪亮，
她为何无限忧伤
人类黑暗而空虚。
理想允尽鲜血

Second Coming

Into this world comes the stranger
Weeping.
            It has happened before –
The arrival of the Wise men
Frightening innocent birds,
The stable, the starry night above,
The infinite sorrow of mother-love
For mankind, bleak and dark –

The Son of God, all over again.

地图

翻开心灵的地图册
全是深渊与忧伤
星星—孤独—月亮—忧郁—太阳—疯狂

秋天灰暗的尽头。孤独的乌鸦
闪电与灰烬
天际暴露的黑暗已经成熟

大地上不幸的豹。
病危的马。沉默的鹰随时覆灭
幽灵跳舞。

旅行者的一生，停在旅途中
女妖穿越阴暗的湿地找你。哭泣的鸟
黄昏之上遥远的伤心的爱情

The Map

The map of my heart,
If you read it right,
Is full of canyons, sorrows,

Crows in autumn,
Lightings and ashes,
Skylines blackening, growing clearer,

Leopards and horses
Hunted, starved,
An eagle vanishing into its sky,

A traveler's swampland, the love-cry
Of a bird at evening
Reaching you.

港口

港口埋藏着多少绝望的沉船？
崩溃的天空，孤儿在最瘦弱的时候死去

天使哭了
我跟着天使哭了

政客的眼睑被卵虫纠缠
大地荒芜和往年一样沉寂

绵羊挤满光滑的岛屿，被恶人反复诅咒
它们不肯死也不肯堕落

世界变亮呀
上帝站在外面

The Harbour

An angel weeps, as I weep
For the sunk boat underwater,
The sky collapsing,
The dead orphan, his hollowed cheeks.

As usual, the barren land
Has its potentates, its parasites,
Its crowds of the innocent

Neither dead nor depraved,
Cursed by the wicked –
An island among islands

Lit by a ray of divinity.

城市麻雀

贩卖玫瑰的小孩
游荡在温暖腐烂的都市的傍晚
蝙蝠废除蓝色的洞穴
米饭的香气勾着他们饥饿的幻觉
海鲜和啤酒的泡沫回荡在妓女的胃里

花朵脏了，在夏季尖叫
河畔树枝上的麻雀
他们幼小的阴影，被黄昏抚摸
母鹿烦闷的坐在餐馆前
动物为何被标上出售的标记

Urban Jungle

Children, peddling roses, drift about
On a sultry evening, in this city
Of bats and ruins, where fragrance of cooked rice,
Piled plates of seafood, foaming beer,
Are the soul's and the streetwalker's asking price.

The great unwashed, like flowers in dirt
Scream at each other on hot summer nights.
The sparrows, happy criminals,
Dust themselves down, on the river bank.
Eaters or eaten, which are the animals?

孤山

送葬队伍在原地
转头鼻子通红
殉难者回到孤寂的故地
我的时代单调，
五十种消炎药
牙痛折磨着下颌神经
大地埋藏了多少孤儿
在阴暗的炉子上
时光化为水蒸气
理想是湿透了的碎纸
无法飘起却沾满秋天的小径

Lone Mountain

The millions of dead
Unlamented, the grieving turned away,
The deportees going back to their homelands
To make their own hay
Give way, now, to an age
Of painkillers, antibiotics,
General anaesthesia.
Quick, turn the page
On orphans buried underground,
Ideals lying around
Like autumn leaves, or scraps of paper
Waiting for a wind.

呐喊

我填饱了肚子，因此可以呐喊。
在城市游走。
需要思考吗。

眼神藏在厚厚的镜片之后，你知道，却依旧犀利。

你是贫困潦倒的诗人，
思想如此丰沛。
我想唱出一首歌，才能画出那纠缠的思维。

今天的山看上去特别远
天空和狮子死了，虚弱的生命畏缩在角落
神啊！你究竟要考验良知多少年？

屠夫踩着鲜花而来，谎言下面压着更多的谎言
千年的白骨压着万年的白骨

死亡前的死亡像干枯无用的草
雨水擦去玻璃上的祖国

The Scream

Wandering as I do, with a full belly,
An empty mind, through the remnants of this city,
Have I the right to let out a scream?

Anyone looking at me
Might see, behind my thickened lenses,
Tricks of light, the sudden sharpened glance,

And say to me 'Dear poet,
Frustrated, penniless, thoughts a mere jingle,
Hide your complexity for another day'.

The mountains, today, are far in the distance,
Ideals, like lion or sun, have failed,
Lives out of breath lie curled up at the corners,

And the blossoms, proffered in peace,
Lie trodden on, the lies beneath lies
Are buried, the martyrs' bones beneath martyrs' bones

And the years of trial, how many times
Relived by conscience, where armies
Goose-stepped over blossoms, and the grasses

Withered, deaths before death,
And the rain came, washing from the windows
The image of a mother country.

葱和生姜

——50年前一份泣血菜单

忘记辅料，必死于非命
炖牛肉煨羊肉猪头肉猪耳朵
猪舌头猪尾巴炖黄豆
猪蹄萝卜汤南京老鸭汤鸭血粉丝汤
扬州老鹅贵阳鸡汤
蒸咸带鱼鲜鲳鱼
整条鳜鱼鲫鱼豆腐汤
白蒸青鱼不再煎熬不再煎熬
黄鳝逃了网袋里是鳗鱼和甲鱼
香肠腊肠红肠肝和肫
蛋饺蒸蛋咸蛋蛋炒饭
肉圆咸肉红烧肉骨头喂乌狗
腊肉腊肉腊肉腊肉
昨天。腊肉嵌进牙缝。
牙床糜烂坏死。留下空洞的牙根
黑暗的嘴吞噬烈酒。你烈
别忘记辅料，你必死于非命
猪油！猪油！猪油！猪油！
猪头。猪头。猪头。

Scallion and Ginger

menu for haemolacria, 50 years ago

Essential
Leave out the spice, or death will be violent

Optional
Stewed beef, simmered lamb, pig's ear
The snout of a groundhog smothered with sauce
Pig's tongue and tail stewed with soybeans
Radish soup, pig's trotters
Soup of old duck from Nanking
Duck's blood soup, glass noodles
Old goose of Yangchow, chicken soup of Guiyang
Pomfret, steamed and salted ribbonfish,
Crucian and bean curd soup
Steamed herring (humanely steamed)
Soft-shell turtle, trapped
Where the eels fled through the meshes

Meatballs and bacon, braised pork
Bones of sacrificial dog
Pork between teeth, for the gum erosions
And the holes in speech, the dark lips
Gulping down strong liquor
Pig's heads, pig's heads for the pig-headed!

Reminder
Leave out the spice, or death will be violent

乌鸦

岁月摧毁苍老的灵魂
狂怒的乌鸦使天空暗淡
卡车和房屋转移在空阔的大地上
在冰雪覆盖的下陷处
一个孤单的小巢
我躲藏其中得知远处有圣火
也许我只是破碎的陨石
或一只飞散的云雀
沙哑得太久而忘记发音

The Crow

Which grows older, the soul itself
Or the age bulldozing the soul?
On the barren fields, houses and traffic
Come into being and scatter again
Like a flock of anxious crows
Against eternity. Am I the last
In my lonely nest, on the snow-covered edge
Of whatever town, to see which way
The wind blows, and the direction of fire?
I, the last of the carrion birds,
A prophet, a corrupter of words.

疾病像光

当出租车司机的脸，
像被反复拧过的水果
他脸上的血管堵塞了
心脏跳在计价器上
"你不知道这个时代的道路
多么拥挤，多少难走"
因为生活像一场疾病被堵在半途
追不上远去的医生

Crosstown Traffic

The taxi-driver's screwed-up face
Like a squeezed fruit, a concentrate
Of blocked veins, troubled heart-rate
Logged on the meter, turns and says
'You have no idea how hard the roads are –
Crosstown traffic, blockage, power ...'
A wounded physician, driving me
To the clinic of souls, the surgery.

是非

舌头软如莲花，传递热与渴望
慈爱、善辨、狡黠、曲直
某个愚昧而纯朴的民族
她寻找唇，嘴里之爱
如火焰燃烧着，耗尽伤痛
她不停地说话，实际上想沉默

Right and Wrong

Lotus flower, your tongues of flame,
Desire and rhetoric, cunning, violence,
Corrupt you, like a crowd inflamed
By nationhood, deaf to its own past
Listening, as a liar shouts
On a platform, in a pantomime of silence.

红焖鲤鱼

她在火焰里游动。瞬间疯了
我想摁住一个词：涟漪
鱼头熟了，鱼尾还在喜剧般摆动
忘记一切。包括忘记幸福
酷刑消灭肉体
它没有被烧红而是被焖红

Braised Carp

The word, like a braised carp,
Undergoes slow mutation
On the griddle. Tragicomically
The tail flaps, while the head is ready
For consumption. Is it dead, then,
The word, after so long a torture,
Or is it something left behind
Like a braised carp, in the mind?

诅咒

―献给曼杰尔斯塔姆

我诅咒你却还是景仰你
你被恶人陷害却继续称颂他们的人性

你在垃圾里寻找食物
却毕生称颂自由

你带走爱情、名誉、欢乐
却未能带走噩梦

Curse

to Mandelstam

Mandelstam, hero of mine,
You drank from Russia's poisoned chalice
But also its finest wine.

Unnoticed, ever-present,
One with the crowd, you sifted common life
For freedom, moral essence.

Happiness, fame and love
Eternally yours ... and ours the nightmare
This side of the grave.

After

桶

我有一个漆成红色的桶,
被遗忘在北京
我说探它的那一次，看到我的脸在水里晃动

当我得知邪恶会永久伴随人类善良只能化作泪水滴落桶中

它被洪水冲上岸时,
阳光穿透它的裂缝它被神秘的洋流挟裹到天际,
大海试图把它托起

你不必惊讶于黑暗过早地到来它从未离开你的四周

The Bucket

The bucket I owned, and left behind in Beijing,
Was painted red. In its hollow darkness
Staring once, I saw my face in the water –

Humanity, blackened by vice,
Virtue, dissolving in a meltdown of tears.

Illumination, when it's washed ashore,
Will leak through its many holes.
Waves will keep it afloat, against ocean currents.

Before I get over the early onset of nightfall,
Darkness will swallow it up.

幻想

那个人生活在幻想的城市里
他看见街，街就是他的
他看见房子，房子也是他的

他看见鸽子，就飞起来
飞出寂静的窗子
他飞到天堂，头脑里飘着许多云

Illusion

A man dwells in an illusory city.
If he sees streets, the streets belong to him.
If he sees houses, the houses are his.

And as for the pigeons ... he wings his way skywards
Through the silence of a window
Mind-devoured, to a heaven of weightlessness.

恐惧

有一个人坐在家里十分恐惧
他写诗时，想到死亡

妻子站在身后，他一转身
妻子变成了秋天

秋天和他吵架，他弹着钢琴
跑来很多怪兽

Fear

A man sits at home, fear-stricken.
Death occurs to him as he writes his poem.

His wife is standing at his back.
She turns into autumn as soon as he looks around.

Autumn, death – himself at his private keyboard,
Demons crowding behind.

魔鬼在今夜复活

黑暗坐在光明的怀里
野花摇晃着大地

魔鬼提着地狱的铁笼，在大地上走来走去

鱼返回宽阔的海洋
鸟站在比道德更高的树枝

魔鬼提着地狱的铁笼，捉拿它不顺眼的人

死亡抢劫了理想
留下'噗'的一声

Tonight the Demon Awakens

The demon steals into the arms of lovers.
Wildflowers try to break new ground.

The demon carries the Purgatory cage around.
The demon is making free.

Fish in the ocean dive for shelter.
Birds on branches perch above morality.

The demon carries the cage from Purgatory,
Harassing the unholy.

Death, where the lungs no longer cope,
Has put an end to hope.

花

你的脸变形后，红色变成白色

花在喉咙深处，没有出路的风暴

花回旋在胸腔内
擦亮你全身并空旷

花留下粉色紫色褐色裂缝
冰凉的脊椎从中年挺到晚年

Carnation

The image of your face, distorted –
Red cheeks turning pale.

Petals deep in your throat,
Storm-shelterers, with no escape.

Petals like lung-trees in your chest,
Petals the void scatters, an offering on your corpse.

Petals leaving space behind, old purples and browns,
And a frozen stalk
That holds from midlife into dotage.

酒徒之夜

这一夜，我睡在酒里
所有故乡都是孤零零的
所有人朝天堂飞去

月亮的大船，把我送往黑暗的港口
不知何处扔下我
埋葬我，只要一杯

睡在酒里，世界杳无人迹

Drinker's Night

Tonight I doze in liquor,
Desertion my home.
Everyone makes his own way,
All roads lead to Rome.

Moonshine my landfall
Harbour of darkness, nowhere going,
Bury me, at one with the earth,
Place beside me one more glass

Like a nightlight, glowing.

杨炼

幽居的杨炼，在坡上村写史诗
他随手扔掉云的花床单
从不去礼堂看明星义演

钢琴飘进他脑子里，他不会写进诗里
他只爱骷髅、面具、看幽灵跳舞
疯狂的用中文写诗，写了很多史诗

蚊子缠着他，要喝血
帝王缠着他，要复活
女人缠着他，要摸瀑布的头发

To Yang Lian

Isolated, an outcast,
Sitting on hillsides scribbling verse,
Turning his back on floral bed linen,
Paying no visits to charity galas.

Incantation wrecking his head,
Unwritten lines of poetry –
Skeletons doing the foxtrot, death in disguise,
Hysterical laughter, lies …

Mosquitoes his fan-club, sucking blood,
Emperors killing him, for revivals,
Women seducing him, that time may spare
The beauty, at least, of their long hair.

让我

让我别再因情欲而抛弃肉体
你根本不存在
让我成为一个圣徒
让我能否找到自己的缺陷和阴影
我的心开始下雨

现在是冬季，让我想想春天
我在冰川边缘漫游
让我理解肉体深处是否有爱
用什么词能准确表达爱

Let Me ...

Let me not abandon my body
To lust, if that exists.
Let me be a saint
Whose weakness and whose shadow move
In a carnal mist.

It's winter now. It's raining
In heartspace. I think of Spring
And edge around my interior glacier.
If I correctly understand,
Love may appear in bottomless lust.
So which should I defend?

一天

经过一个很响的湖。
我两手空空，没有得到任何东西。

我甚至没有出声。
鱼是哑巴，跳来跳去像一把刀。

我们说：时间消逝，其实是自己消逝。
时间本身在衰老。
比如荒芜的一天。

One Day

Empty-handed, nothing gained,
I passed by the teeming lake of life.

Instead of clamour, silent surface
Broken by one dumb fish, like a knife.

Time disappears, we say,
When it is we ourselves who disappear
Like this random, wasted day.

幻灭

我在蓝色的夜晚去找幽灵
为了请教威胁与死亡的来源
这并不是藉口

我还想知道道德的等级
她犹豫了，什么话都不说
远处的河流传来泛滥的响声

Disillusion

I asked the furies, in the deep blue night,
Where are the roots of fear and death?
Asking, I gained no forgiveness.

I tried to plead the case for morality.
They held back, saying nothing,
But from afar, approached a swollen river ...

爱之痛

麻风病人在凌晨跳舞
你出生。不是情欲是神的创造
庸俗商人是城市最大的买主

穷人的孩子最爱甜食
神厌烦的时候，我代替她思考
我和飞禽漫游四海，见惯了人间的一切
狮子是晴朗的高原睡眠，人类喝酒也喝血
天使和星星照亮爱的伤口

Out of Love

Twinned together, opposites danced
The night of your conception –
You, no fruit of Eros but divinity.

Dirty dealers the chosen buyers of your city,
Children of the poor the stealers of your sweets.

In a godless time, you play the role of the wise.
You jet through the skies, like a bird of prey
Witnessing, beneath you, mortal existence.

Human beast, you sleep on your plateau
Of achievement, wine-drinker,
Blood-sucker, sunlit,
Starlit, in and out of love.

城市

你总是炫耀你的过去，我却反复走入同一条河流。
踏上陌生之城，为了寻求新的梦境。
这里比那里好。却和那里一样空。

我的命运一直被推搡着往后退，
面具戴得太久已和脸上的血肉粘连
那些尸体早已被埋葬，依然还是尸体。

在不同的荒蛮之地，靠什么支撑理想？

The City

To you the past, but to me
The eternal present, repeatedly
At large in the same city,
Only the imaginings different.

The dead and buried
Are who they always were,
But I, unrecognisable
To myself, in a social mask,
Carry out my nefarious tasks.

Different city, different name –
Disenchantment always the same.

酒馆

酒馆是暴风的终点，麻痹自己只是一个借口
只有从沉醉中清醒，你才像人

幽灵撕去世界的面具
理想在半途弯曲

世上没有完全对称的王冠
你只是一个灵魂永远是一个灵魂

Public House Blues

Drunkenness, Sturm und Drang –
A whimper not a bang

As the ham actor chickens out,
His bluster in doubt,

His crown askew,
His paltry ego in view.

休士顿，请别哭泣

女妖天使脱衣舞。病人在病中尤感寂寞
音乐酿制的红酒味道酸甜
我在秋夜思念你

老友，你过得如何

两只猫还在你的眼前
与修女还交往吗
我想送你棕色的提琴

Don't Cry, Houston

Enchantress, angel, striptease –
Where the weak man is abandoned,
Where music, well-aged wine,
Leave a strange taste in the mouth –
I miss you, on this autumn night.

Old friend, how have you been?
Are the two cats still with you?
Are you still dating a nun?
Does the light blue brush
Remember me, and the brown violin?

秘密生活

黑暗的四周没有动静

一个醒着的人坐着，与容量突然跌在他脸上
他们坐在脸上
矿工们坐在很远的地方

他想咽下月亮
人群涌上街道，妇女们去买菜了
他跌落在月光下

天鹅突然变得灰暗的时候，他们调转方向
先朝东又朝南飞。他坐着
看着蝴蝶化为灰烬

Secret Life

Silence, surrounding darkness.

Moonlight wanes, and dissipates.
Awake, he sits up straight,
A stranger to his own depths,

Gulping moonshine, still half-drunk
On visions of crowds in busy streets,
Women in markets, himself
Moonstruck, stumbling home …

A thunder of swans going east and south,
An after-image of butterfly-women
Greying into cigarette ash.

随 想

恶人被凌迟，额头叮着苍蝇
野兽在宋朝蹭着兽性的腰
你在天堂旅行，回家时已经是一个天使

大地把着头弓身睡在风暴下
人类不知去向
出逃的动物挤满云朵

Golgotha

A criminal crucified,
Forehead covered with flies,
Ascends to heaven,
Returns as an angel

To earth, in a windstorm
Of animals, men in crowds,
The lost travellers
Between death and resurrection.

但丁

盗贼与蛇从他脚下逃走
还有伪造金币者，贩卖假货者
肮脏的嫖客，廉价的妓女
邪恶的施暴邻居的人
但丁在天堂看着静如一只巨鹰
孩子们在他头脑里
火红的大鸟。飞越河流
悲剧的琴弦为迷路人弹奏晚祷的歌
但丁手掩长袍，搀扶他年迈的老师
看着地狱里那只新来的大鸟

Dante

Traffickers, crime syndicates,
Women with bare breasts,
Petty thieves and money-changers,
Weird heraldic beasts –

He sees them all, a bird's-eye view
Eternities long, who crossed
Ahead of time the burning Styx,
The river of the lost,

Who hides himself behind the robe
Of Virgil, as a bat out of hell
Comes riding the updraught
With a future to foretell.

AFTERWORD

The movement of texts across language and place, and what we do or do not get from those texts is older probably than Zoroaster, whose deciphered characters sat for centuries in the monasteries of western China, supposedly originating a whole religious worldview in those regions, remote to us but not to themselves. Were the words, the meanings faithful, or was it all an inspired misunderstanding, which nonetheless comforts those who believe, or need to?

Much later, though still in China, the question remains when we engage, as I first did in adolescence, with the strangely beautiful texts by Ezra Pound in his *Cathay* collection of renderings from classical Chinese poems as literally translated by Arthur Waley. Are we anywhere close to the spirit and substance of an original, and does it matter? Robert Lowell, half a century later, declared that faithful translators were no more than taxidermists producing stuffed animals, and handed over his wildly subjective renderings of European texts to an apprehensive T.S.Eliot, who suggested 'versions' rather than 'translations' might be more appropriate. In the event, they were published, to some controversy, as 'Imitations'.

I myself, at the beginning of the seventies, lived through a short but influential age of poetry translation, in which a previously unmapped zone of feeling and experience, that of Russia and Eastern Europe, was introduced to the west in a series called Penguin Modern European Poets in Translation. The effect on the rather staid Anglo-Saxon poetic imagination was electric, though I suspect the translations, in the purely technical sense, were rudimentary. Not that it mattered. Something larger, a moral essence of sorts, was being brought across. Imagination, occasioned by need, filled in the spaces.

And so to Yau Noi. Who is he? A modern Chinese poet, a set of shapes on a page, with a moving shadow behind them, re-imagining himself, as we all do, out of childhood anguish, immersion in love and history, and the backward look of later age. Before, during, and after. All poetry, even in the mother tongue, translates or tries to from that moving shadow, that silence on the other side of language itself – be it Yau Noi, Liu Xun or the present writer – or, more likely, the compound ghost of all three.

— Harry Clifton

ABOUT THE TRANSLATORS

Xun Liu is currently pursuing her Ph.D. degree in linguistics at Trinity College Dublin; her research mainly looks at cognitive metaphors in Chinese vernacular novels of the 18th century. She is a freelance literary and academic translator in her free time. Her interests lie in Chinese modern poetry and academic publication on Chinese classical literature. Xun is also engaged in giving public lectures about Chinese vernacular novels and the literary history of the High-Qing period.

Harry Clifton is one of the best-known of his generation of Irish poets. *The Holding Centre: Selected Poems 1974–2004* was published in 2014, and *Ireland and its Elsewheres,* his lectures as Ireland Professor of Poetry, in 2015. More recently, he has published *Portobello Sonnets* (2016) and *Herod's Dispensations* (2019). He teaches at Trinity College Dublin and is a member of Aosdána, the affiliation of creative artists in Ireland.

www.ingramcontent.com/pod-product-compliance
Lightning Source LLC
LaVergne TN
LVHW091226080426
835509LV00009B/1186